'This is a remarkab

and compelling, aut

the glories of Calvai

He reminds us that all the Old Testament ultimately points to Christ by walking through Psalm 22 as it unfolds both Christ's death and resurrection. I could not put the book down, and as I raced to the finish, I was filled with joy, which Mallard reminds us comes not from performance but from proximity. Read this book as it will help you gaze at Christ's love and remind you that Jesus is our sure and steady anchor.'

Dave Furman, Senior Pastor, Redeemer Church of Dubai and author of *Being There*

'These are wonderful meditations on the Cross and Resurrection of Christ through the lens of Psalm 22. We are invited to reflect in a fresh way on Christ. More than that, we see that the sufferings and glory of Christ provide the keys to our own Christian life and experience. Spiritually refreshing!'

Bill James, Principal, London Seminary

'Paul Mallard guides us skilfully through Psalm 22, tracing Christ's suffering at Calvary and the triumph of his resurrection, inviting us to meditate on the Saviour's love for sinners and his passion for God's glory. The victory cry, "He has done it" points to Christ's supremacy, leads us to worship and infuses our faith with hope. This short book is packed with rich treasure.'

Elizabeth McQuoid, Digital Resources Director, Keswick Ministries

'Christ-exalting; heart-warming; soul-nourishing; perspective-giving; praise-provoking. This walk-through Psalm 22 affirms the fact that the cross and resurrection of our Lord Jesus truly are the anchor for our souls. This short book is like a pair of glasses that enable us to focus afresh on the sufferings of Jesus and the glories that would follow. We see other things more clearly as we fix our thoughts on the Pioneer and Perfecter of our faith.'

Johnny Prime, Director for London of the Fellowship of Independent Evangelical Churches (FIEC)

AN ANCHOR FOR THE SOUL

Beholding the cross and resurrection

PAUL MALLARD

10 Publishing
a division of 10 of those.com

For Bruce, thank you for your friendship:
'Well done, good and faithful servant.'

First published in Great Britain in 2024

British Library Cataloguing in Publication Data
A record for this book is available from the British Library

ISBN: 978-1-915705-33-4

Designed and typeset by Pete Barnsley (CreativeHoot.com)

Printed in Denmark

10Publishing, a division of 10ofthose.com
Unit C, Tomlinson Road, Leyland, PR25 2DY, England

Email: info@10ofthose.com
Website: www.10ofthose.com

1 3 5 7 10 8 6 4 2

CONTENTS

Introduction:
WHEN I SURVEY

We can all remember a sermon that has had a profound effect on us.

For me, that occasion was when I was in my late teens and attending a Christian conference with other members of our youth group. The sermon that evening was engaging, but I don't think that I had particularly connected with the message until the speaker reached his conclusion:

> *A few years ago, I was preaching in India. There were huge crowds and I had to speak through an interpreter. The young man was very gifted and we had a great rapport.*
>
> *I was there over Easter, and on Good Friday I was preaching about the cross of Jesus. I was*

> *speaking and my friend was interpreting. Everything was going well.*
>
> *I came to the point where I was beginning to describe the suffering of Jesus. I paused and waited for the interpretation to follow. Nothing happened. Perhaps I had spoken too quickly? So I repeated my last sentence. Still no interpretation. When nothing happened after a third try, I looked at this young Christian brother.*
>
> *He was in tears. He was choked up. He could not speak. A fresh sight of Calvary love had gripped his heart. His heart had been smitten and his love had been rekindled.*

Then the preacher paused, as preachers often do.

> *How about you today? Do you love Christ as you did at first? Does he still move your heart? Are you still amazed at grace? If not, go back to the cross and gaze again at the wonders of Calvary love.*

God spoke to me that night. I remembered my first sight of the cross and longed for the freshness of that first love.

We all know how easy it is for us to drift. We need an anchor. The cross and resurrection of Christ provide such an anchor.

When I was growing up, my pastor would regularly take us to the cross of Jesus and beyond that to his glorious resurrection. With tears in his eyes, he would urge us to never lose sight of Jesus Christ: 'Whatever you face in this life, Jesus, his cross and his empty tomb are the answer.' How right he was!

Sometimes our love for Jesus grows cold and our faith seems to be a mere formality. Yet we wear a mask to hide the deadness of our hearts. Diligent in our religion, we are distant in our relationship.

On other occasions we flirt with sin and fall into its vice-like grip. Overwhelmed with a sense of guilt and worthlessness, we wonder how God could ever love failures like us. We find ourselves on a treadmill as we try somehow to earn God's approval, but never quite meet our self-imposed targets.

Or maybe pain and grief have invaded our lives and stamped a dark question mark over our faith. We question why a loving God would treat us so badly.

If you have ever been in any of these places, Jesus, his cross and his empty tomb *are* the answer.

The purpose of this little book is to take us back to Calvary and to the empty tomb so that we gaze again at the mystery of grace and the profundity of love poured out for us there. Our joy in Christ comes not from performance but from proximity.

We could approach our subject in a variety of ways. I have chosen to focus on the cross and resurrection through the lens of Psalm 22. In what follows, we will see how the psalm was perfectly fulfilled in the life of Jesus. Beyond that, we will discover how amazingly relevant and vital its message is for us today. Here is an anchor for our souls that will give us stability through the raging tempests of life.

After all, the events of Jesus' death and resurrection were not an afterthought – they were in the mind of the triune God before the creation of the world. Revealed in prophecy and accomplished in history, they are now the theme of our worship as well as the anchor for our souls.

Come back with me to a thousand years before the cross and see how God shared his secrets with King David.

1

FINDING OUR WAY TO CALVARY

Three simple questions

I became an RE teacher in 1978. In those days, there was still a strong emphasis on the Gospels. Most kids were familiar with the significance of Christmas and Easter, and had a rudimentary knowledge of the life and teaching of Jesus. Sadly, today, much of that has gone with the wind. But back in the seventies, if you talked about the cross and the resurrection to children, they would understand.

Each year, just before Easter, I would print out Psalm 22 and give it to my RE class of thirteen- and fourteen-year-olds. There was nothing on the handout identifying either the author or the context of the passage. Along with the text, I posed three questions:

1. What is this passage about?
2. When do you think it was written?
3. Who do you think wrote it?

For the five years that I taught, these questions produced very similar answers:

1. 'It's about Jesus dying on the cross.' Not everyone understood this truth – and very few identified the fact that the passage goes on to speak of the resurrection – but the story of Good Friday was known well enough for most children to get the right answer.
2. There was less unanimity about question two. Some of the children thought that it might have been written almost immediately after Calvary since it contains so many details. Other answers ranged from five years to fifty years after Jesus' death. Where they were all in agreement

was that it obviously must have been written after the events of Good Friday.

3. Answers to the last question ranged from Peter to Paul to John. I guess that these were the only names they could remember. The majority of the pupils had no idea and said so! What they did agree on was that whoever wrote the passage must have been an eyewitness since the details are so precise.

The references to the cross in Psalm 22 are unmissable:

All who see me mock me;
they hurl insults, shaking their heads.
'He trusts in the LORD,' they say,
'let the LORD rescue him.
Let him deliver him,
since he delights in him.' (Verses 7–8)

Dogs surround me,
a pack of villains encircles me;
they pierce my hands and my feet.
All my bones are on display;

people stare and gloat over me.
They divide my clothes among them
and cast lots for my garment. (Verses 16–18)

In addition, if you read the Gospel accounts of Jesus' death, you will discover that they are saturated with the whole of this psalm.

Back to my RE lesson. After everyone agreed that this psalm was about Jesus, I would give out copies of the Bible and get the class to turn to Psalm 22. While the psalm is about the cross, it is also about the resurrection. But what is most remarkable is that it was written by King David over a thousand years before the events it describes with such clarity, detail and precision. Perhaps even more amazing, it was written almost five hundred years before the first recorded example of a crucifixion. David was not describing something which he had witnessed. Indeed, he was describing something which no one had witnessed before.

Like most people when presented with the miraculous nature of the Bible, some of the kids were amazed, others were sceptical and most were totally indifferent.

One remarkable psalm

Like a third of the psalms, Psalm 22 has elements of lament in it. Mark Vroegop puts it like this:

> *Lament is how we bring our sorrow to God. Without lament we won't know how to process pain. Silence, bitterness, and even anger can dominate our spiritual lives instead.*
>
> *Lament is how Christians grieve. It is how to help hurting people. Lament is how we learn important truths about God and our world.*[1]

As a typical lament, Psalm 22 moves from complaint to prayer and on to faith. It flows from a bruised and broken heart. The psalm's historical setting was perhaps when David was being pursued by Saul and felt abandoned by God. But it transcends its context and reaches forward as it predicts the cross of Christ.

There is so much in the psalm which goes way beyond anything which David experienced. Most obviously it culminates in describing the death of the psalmist while he is still very much alive:

> *My mouth is dried up like a potsherd,*
> *and my tongue sticks to the roof of my mouth;*
> *you lay me in the dust of death.* (Verse 15)

In the Gospels, we have four accounts of Jesus' crucifixion. Each is unique and together they lead us to the foot of the cross where we adore our Saviour. In Psalm 22, we have what might be described as a 'fifth Gospel'. Written in poetic language, it directs us to the first Easter. However, it is also unique in that it is a personal account of the sufferings and faith of Jesus. It reveals his heart and is a verbal expression of the sorrows and hopes of his soul. Indeed, as we shall see, Jesus chose this psalm to describe his experiences on the cross. Perhaps he dwelt on the words of the psalm as he trod the lonely road which led to Calvary. He not only quoted the psalm, he lived it.

As a boy, Jesus would have sung the psalms in a synagogue. When did it dawn on him that they were a description of the road that he would have to tread? Did it send a shiver down his spine as he contemplated the intensity of his passion? How did it shape his expectations and mould his obedience? As John Stott explains:

> *From Jesus' youth, indeed even from his birth, the cross cast its shadow ahead of him. His death was central to his mission. Moreover, the church has always recognized this.*[2]

Two clear halves

The psalm moves from darkness to light: from the darkness of pain and death (verses 1–21) to the glorious light of life and exaltation (verses 22–31). A thousand years before Jesus died and rose again, God described in stunning detail events which would bisect history and which would lead to the redemption of a people who would eternally sing his praises. This picture of heaven is further described in the book of Revelation:

> *After this I looked, and there before me was a great multitude that no one could count, from every nation, tribe, people and language, standing before the throne and before the Lamb. They were wearing white robes and were holding palm branches in their hands. And they cried out in a loud voice:*
> *'Salvation belongs to our God,*
> *who sits on the throne,*
> *and to the Lamb.'* (Revelation 7:9–10)

So how does our psalm find fulfilment in the New Testament? One place that echoes it is Paul's profound song of praise describing the humiliation and exaltation of Christ (Philippians 2:5–11). Jesus stoops lower than could be imagined and is then exalted beyond anything that might be anticipated. From the throne of heaven he stoops lower and lower and lower still (as is described in verses 5–8). Without ceasing to be God, he becomes a real man and a servant:

> *And being found in appearance as a man,*
> *he humbled himself*
> *by becoming obedient to death –*
> *even death on a cross!* (Philippians 2:8)

Jesus could not have descended further – crucified people were despised as the scum of the earth. Christ descended to a place of shame and dishonour. He was totally discredited and disgraced.

But then comes the turning point. Having offered himself in faith to his Father, Jesus is raised by the Father from the dust of death and seated at his right hand:

Therefore God exalted him to the highest place
and gave him the name that is
above every name,
that at the name of Jesus every knee should bow,
in heaven and on earth and under the earth,
and every tongue acknowledge that Jesus
Christ is Lord,
to the glory of God the Father.
(Philippians 2:9–11)

Jesus is 'super-exalted' as a reward for his obedience to his Father's will.

Paul may have found the structure for these verses from an early Christian hymn which predates his letter. Perhaps the hymn was directly inspired by Psalm 22, with its identical structure.

One reasonable response

In the light of this, how should we live? What difference should Psalm 22 make to our lives? All our theology, all our discipleship and all our service must be conducted within earshot of Calvary.

Isaac Watts expresses it like this:

Were the whole realm of nature mine,
That were an offering far too small;
Love so amazing, so divine,
Demands my soul, my life, my all.[3]

Watts reminds us in the opening words of his great hymn that we should kneel in wonder before the cross. The apostle Paul adds that if kneeling in adoration is sincere, it will result in a surrendered life:

> *Therefore, I urge you, brothers and sisters, in view of God's mercy, to offer your bodies as a living sacrifice, holy and pleasing to God – this is your true and proper worship.* (Romans 12:1)

God painted a perfect picture of the cost of our salvation centuries before it happened. At one moment in time, on a small hill outside the city of Jerusalem, God carried his purpose through to completion. The young prince of glory offered up his life in fulfilment of prophecy and in obedience to his Father's will. Three days later, he crushed death for ever and triumphed over all his enemies. In the light of this, no sacrifice is too great for us to make for him.

If we engage honestly and humbly with Psalm 22, it will change our lives.

QUESTIONS

1. Jesus was 'the Lamb who was slain from the creation of the world' (Revelation 13:8). Psalm 22 is able to predict the cross because it was in God's mind from eternity. What does this teach us about God? What are the implications for our understanding of the gospel?
2. The greatest distance in the universe is between the throne of heaven and the cross of Calvary. Read Philippians 2:5–11. What are the stages of Christ's descent to the cross? Now read Philippians 2:1–5 and 12–18. What are the practical implications of this for our lives?
3. Jesus is 'the pioneer and perfecter of faith', and 'for the joy that was

set before him he endured the cross, scorning its shame, and sat down at the right hand of the throne of God' (Hebrews 12:2). What does this teach us about the courage, faith and perseverance of Jesus? Read Hebrews 12:1–13. What should we learn from his example?

Part 1

GOOD FRIDAY ANTICIPATED

As we have seen, Psalm 22 falls into two quite distinct parts as it anticipates its eventual fulfilment by Jesus. The first half of the psalm describes Christ's descent into the darkness of grief, pain and torment as he experiences both the hatred of men and the wrath of God on the first Good Friday (verses 1–21). The second half celebrates his resurrection and the expansion of his kingdom, which began on Easter Sunday (verses 22–31).

As we approach the first half of the psalm across the landscape of time, we see Christ's agony and enter into his own perception of what is happening to him. We cannot read and meditate on these words without feeling that we are on holy ground.

Christianity is a religion about a cross. At the heart of the Bible is the life of Christ, and at the heart of the life of Christ is the cross.

The first part of the psalm falls into three distinct sections. They are like three waves that will sweep over Christ as he experiences the horrors of Calvary. In each case, we foresee Jesus' intense suffering and courageous faith as he appeals to God for deliverance and expresses confidence in his Father. Each section is a cry from the heart and will form the substance of the next three chapters:

1. I am forsaken (verses 1–5).
2. I am despised (verses 6–11).
3. I am crucified (verses 12–21).

2

I AM FORSAKEN

For the director of music. To the tune of 'The Doe of the Morning'. A psalm of David.

1 *My God, my God, why have you forsaken me?*
Why are you so far from saving me,
so far from my cries of anguish?
2 *My God, I cry out by day, but*
you do not answer,
by night, but I find no rest.

3 *Yet you are enthroned as the Holy One;*
you are the one Israel praises.
4 *In you our ancestors put their trust;*
they trusted and you delivered them.
5 *To you they cried out and were saved;*

in you they trusted and were not put to shame. (Psalm 22:1–5)

The darkness of the cross

Psalm 22 begins with three questions hurled at heaven:

My God, my God, why have you forsaken me?
Why are you so far from saving me,
so far from my cries of anguish? (Verse 1)

The book of Psalms is full of lament, but none quite as poignant as this. This is the most plaintive and agonising cry in the Bible. There is nothing so raw. It perfectly predicts Jesus' sense of total abandonment after three hours in the darkness. He cries out in anguish, but it seems that God is not listening. Christ longs for salvation, but it is far away. God is silent:

My God, I cry out by day, but you do not answer,
by night, but I find no rest. (Verse 2)

Notice that in these first two verses the psalmist still calls God '*my* God' three times, and yet there is a sense of isolation and abandonment.

It is understandable that Jesus, after all his suffering, would likewise cry with such anguish and distress. But there is more going on here than meets the eye. To understand the full impact of these words we have to turn to the Gospels.

Jesus is crucified at nine o'clock in the morning. For the first three hours the cross is a noisy and busy place. As Jesus hangs in agony, he is surrounded by a cacophony of jeers and taunts. The soldiers who nailed him to the cross, the religious leaders who plotted his death and the thieves being crucified next to him sneer and mock him. Even the passers-by join in the 'fun' (Matthew 27:39–44; Mark 15:29–32; Luke 23:35–39). Up to this point it is almost like any other crucifixion – a common sight throughout the Roman empire.

But at noon, when the sun is at its zenith, everything changes:

> *From noon until three in the afternoon darkness came over all the land.* (Matthew 27:45)

> *It was now about noon, and darkness came over the whole land until three in the*

> *afternoon, for the sun stopped shining. And the curtain of the temple was torn in two.* (Luke 23:44–45)

As it was Passover and the time of the full moon, this was no solar eclipse. It was an act of supernatural intervention. How are we to interpret it? Matthew Henry says, 'The sun had never seen such wickedness as this before and therefore withdrew.'[1] The poet John Donne imagines that the sun stops shining in sympathy for the death of its Creator:

> *What a death were it then to see God die?*
> *It made his own Lieutenant Nature shrink,*
> *It made his footstool crack, and the Sun wink.*[2]

These poetic descriptions are helpful in one sense, but they don't get to the heart of the supernatural darkness of Calvary.

The day of the Lord

In the Bible, darkness is a sign of judgement. The penultimate plague in the land of Egypt was the plague of darkness (Exodus 10:21–29). That was the final calamity before the death of all the firstborn sons of the Egyptians. Likewise, God comes down in the darkness of judgement on the hill of Calvary before the death of his Son.

This theme of the darkness of judgement is taken up by the prophets. Listen to Amos:

> *Woe to you who long*
> *for the day of the* L*ORD*!
> *Why do you long for the day of the* L*ORD*?
> *That day will be darkness, not light.*
> *It will be as though a man fled from a lion*
> *only to meet a bear,*
> *as though he entered his house*
> *and rested his hand on the wall*
> *only to have a snake bite him.*
> *Will not the day of the* L*ORD* *be*
> *darkness, not light –*
> *pitch-dark, without a ray of brightness?*
> (Amos 5:18–20)

The day of the Lord is a day when God pours out his wrath on sinful people. Amos' audience expected it to be a day of deliverance, but it would be a day of judgement, symbolised by darkness.

Later Amos is even more specific:

'In that day,' declares the Sovereign L*ORD*,
'I will make the sun go down at noon
and darken the earth in broad daylight.
I will turn your religious festivals into mourning
and all your singing into weeping.
I will make all of you wear sackcloth
and shave your heads.
I will make that time like mourning for an only son
and the end of it like a bitter day.'
(Amos 8:9–10)

At the cross this wrath of God is poured out as never before. Good Friday is a 'day of the LORD', but the recipient of this holy anger is the pure and sinless Son of God. On the cross he bore the full weight of God's judgement. This explains his cry out of the darkness: 'About three in the afternoon Jesus cried out in a loud voice, "*Eli, Eli, lema sabachthani?*" (which means "My God, my God, why have you forsaken me?")' (Matthew 27:46).

Coming out of the supernatural darkness, Jesus chose the opening words of our psalm to describe his experience.

He who knew no sin

In the darkness of Calvary, God's wrath is poured out on human rebellion and sin. At the cross Christ experiences this wrath firsthand as he becomes the substitute for the sins of all his people. The world's outer darkness corresponds with his inner darkness. The Light of the World is cast into the most profound gloom. In this darkness, 'God made him who had no sin to be sin for us, so that in him we might become the righteousness of God' (2 Corinthians 5:21).

Before the creation of the world, Jesus – the Son of God, and the second person of the Trinity – basked in the eternal embrace and love of his Father. Throughout his life Jesus walked confidently in the grip of this grace. His first and last recorded words, before he rose to life, refer to God as his Father (Luke 2:49; 23:46). Throughout his life he constantly refers to God as his Father, sometimes using the diminutive 'Abba'. He teaches us to address God as our Father. Even in the garden of Gethsemane, under the shadow of the cross and in the midst of terrible pain, Jesus addresses God as 'Abba' (Mark 14:32–36).

But on the cross this intimacy is somehow breached and Jesus' cry from the darkness lacks any sense of his Father's love. For the first time he has experienced the absence of God's presence:

But he was pierced for our transgressions,
he was crushed for our iniquities;
the punishment that brought us
peace was on him,
and by his wounds we are healed.
We all, like sheep, have gone astray,
each of us has turned to our own way;
and the LORD has laid on him
the iniquity of us all. (Isaiah 53:5–6)

Christ died on the cross as a substitute for sinners. Like iron filings drawn to a magnet, Jesus took to himself the guilt of all our sins. God imputed – that is, accredited – the guilt of our sins to Christ, and he, in our place, knew the absolute horror of God's judgement as he bore the punishment that we deserve. Jesus paid fully for all our sins so that God's wrath and righteousness were satisfied. God can now forgive us without compromising his holiness.

But what a mystery it is! How can we understand these things?

- Jesus is God, and yet God the Father is his God.
- On the cross Jesus is somehow forsaken by God, and yet there can never be a breach within the fellowship of the holy Trinity.

How can God be forsaken by God? Charles Cranfield argues that Jesus experienced 'not merely a felt, but a real abandonment by his Father. The paradox is that while this god-forsakenness was utterly real, the unity of the Blessed Trinity was even then unbroken.'[3]

Perhaps we can say no more than this. Instead we should bow in wonder at such an amazing mystery. This is the cost of our salvation! Here theology becomes doxology. As the apostle Paul writes to the church in Rome:

Oh, the depth of the riches of the wisdom and knowledge of God!
How unsearchable his judgments,
and his paths beyond tracing out!

Who has known the mind of the Lord?
Or who has been his counsellor?
Who has ever given to God,
that God should repay them?'
For from him and through him and for him are all things.
To him be the glory for ever! Amen.
(Romans 11:33–36)

The holy God who saves

Throughout Psalm 22, as we consider the way it looks forward to the cross, we find that the anguish of Christ is never the final word. His sufferings are always laced with confident hope. So the raw cries of the first two verses are followed by the confident trust of the next three verses:

Yet you are enthroned as the Holy One;
you are the one Israel praises.
In you our ancestors put their trust;
they trusted and you delivered them.
To you they cried out and were saved;
in you they trusted and were not put to shame. (Verses 3–5)

Even in his darkest hour, Jesus knows that God is on the throne. The cross is not an unforeseen disaster. Jesus is not a good man who died tragically young. Everything that happened was planned in eternity, predicted in time and played out on Calvary. Later Peter asserted:

> *This man was handed over to you by God's deliberate plan and foreknowledge; and you, with the help of wicked men, put him to death by nailing him to the cross.* (Acts 2:23)

If the darkest moment in the history of the world was part of God's plan, this should give us confidence in any dark providence that we may have to face. As we lament, we too can move from honest complaint to confident prayer.

In verse 3 of the psalm, God is addressed as the 'Holy One'. Likewise, the prophet Isaiah, out of his experience of God's awesome holiness (Isaiah 6:1–3), constantly refers to God as the 'Holy One' of Israel (Isaiah 43:3, 15; 48:17). He is majestic in holiness – set apart from his creation and utterly unique (Exodus 15:11). At the same time he is utterly pure, so he hates anything which is impure or opposed to his holy nature. He is light and in him is no darkness at all (1 John 1:5). It is terrifying to fall into the hands of the living God (Hebrews 10:31).

God always acts consistently with his character. This means that there are things which he cannot do. He cannot lie and he cannot deny himself (Titus 1:2; Hebrews 6:18; 2 Timothy 2:13). And he cannot sin. Indeed his holy response to sin is wrath or divine anger. Unlike human wrath, this is not capricious, uncontrolled or irrational. It is not malicious, vindictive or spiteful. John Stott writes, 'It is the steady, unrelenting, unremitting, uncompromising antagonism to evil in all its forms and manifestations.'[4] God is slow to anger and abundant in mercy, but one day his wrath will be poured out on sinful people. 'Whoever rejects the Son will not see life, for God's wrath *remains* on them' (John 3:36, my emphasis).

On the cross Jesus tasted this wrath for sinners. The necessity of the cross lay in the character of God and the need to propitiate his wrath. John Piper writes:

> *The substitute, Jesus Christ, does not just cancel the wrath; he absorbs it and drives it*

from us to himself. God's wrath is just and it was spent, not withdrawn.[5]

We are saved by an act of the triune God:

Moved by the perfection of his holy love, God in Christ substituted himself for us sinners. That is the heart of the Cross of Christ.[6]

Peace with God

Every sinner can now cry to God for mercy on the basis of Christ's death, and will then experience forgiveness and be at peace with God. All God's wrath is already spent. We who trust in Jesus come into an unending and warm relationship with our heavenly Father. Like Old Testament believers who cried out and were saved, and who trusted and were not put to shame (Psalm 22:5), we can have absolute confidence in God. As Alistair Begg summarises:

In the cross God has satisfied his perfect and holy justice by executing the punishment our sins deserve. Without that he would not be himself. And in the cross he pardons those who believe in Christ, even though they have sinned and deserve condemnation.[7]

Everyone who truly flees to Christ for salvation is forgiven – totally, unconditionally and eternally. There is now no condemnation for those who are in Christ Jesus. When I sin yet again and feel that there is no way back, I need to look at Jesus. When Satan tempts me to despair, I need to return to the cross. When fear or doubt or pain almost overwhelm me, I need to remember that Jesus experienced the darkness of rejection so that I will never be deserted by my loving Father.

I heard the story once of a little girl who was allergic to bee stings. They were fatal to her. So her parents took great care to protect her. Doors and windows at home were hermetically sealed, creating a bee-free zone. One day after they had put their daughter to bed, they heard a scream of terror from upstairs. Somehow a bee had managed to breach their defences. Dad sprinted into her bedroom and the little girl ran into his arms. Sure enough there was the sinister buzz of a renegade bee. Dad hugged his daughter as closely as he could, protecting her from danger.

In his firm embrace, she suddenly felt him wince. Then he relaxed.

'Everything is fine now. You are safe,' he declared.

To prove his words, he held out his hand. In his palm the girl saw the remains of the bee's sting. To protect his daughter, Dad had deliberately taken the sting himself.

In the darkness of the cross, Christ absorbed the wrath of God in our place. He took the fatal sting which we deserved so that we would be free from condemnation.

Jesus would have read Psalm 22 as a child. He lived his life under its shadow. Knowing what awaited him after the Last Supper, Luke 22:44 describes his sweat like great drops of blood falling to the ground. And yet Jesus still set his face to go to the cross and fulfil the words of the psalm. As he hung in agony, he used the words of the psalm to explain his experience.

Jesus was motivated by unswerving fidelity to his Father and total self-giving love for sinners. What courage! What trust! What love! What a Saviour!

QUESTIONS

- How does Christ's sense of abandonment help us when we feel that God is not listening to our prayers and is far from us?
- Read Mark 14:32–36. What insights does it give to Jesus' understanding of the cross?
- Life can be difficult and we are sometimes tempted to doubt God's love for us. How does dwelling on the cross straighten out our thinking? (John 3:16; 1 John 3:16; 4:10).

3

I AM DESPISED

6 *But I am a worm and not a man,*
scorned by everyone, despised by the people.
7 *All who see me mock me;*
they hurl insults, shaking their heads.
8 *'He trusts in the Lord,' they say,*
'let the Lord rescue him.
Let him deliver him,
since he delights in him.'

9 *Yet you brought me out of the womb;*
you made me trust in you, even at my
mother's breast.
10 *From birth I was cast on you;*
from my mother's womb you have been my God.
11 *Do not be far from me,*

for trouble is near
and there is no one to help. (Psalm 22:6–11)

'I am a worm'

Psalm 22:6–11 predicts the shame that Jesus would experience on the cross. Like the first section of the psalm, it begins with lament as David describes the tidal wave of scorn and contempt that would wash over Jesus (verses 6–8). But amid this anguish there is an amazing statement of confidence in God (verses 9–11).

Look at how this section begins:

But I am a worm and not a man,
scorned by everyone, despised by the people.

The speaker has just expressed his trust in God (verse 5), but now he returns to the magnitude of his suffering. As he contemplates the disgraceful humiliation he is experiencing, he compares himself to a worm. He has been totally dehumanised. He considers himself like the lowest of creatures that is thoughtlessly trampled underfoot. Worms are treated with contempt. Under the Old Testament law, they defile the things they touch. Like maggots they are associated with the corruption of a dead body (Isaiah 14:11). There is nothing noble or winsome about a worm! But this is what Jesus is reduced to on the cross.

And yet the one who ultimately speaks these words is the Lord of glory. He is the one who is utter perfection, boundless in power and of infinite worth. On the cross he sets aside his glory and appears less than human, as low as the lowest of creatures, to redeem rebels like us. The Creator of hundreds of billions of galaxies did this for us!

In memorable words Spurgeon draws out the full implications of the metaphor:

> *This verse is a miracle of language … What a contrast between the 'I am' and 'I am a worm'! He felt himself to be comparable to a helpless, powerless, down-trodden worm, passive while crushed and unnoticed and despised by those who trod upon him.*[1]

The one who declares 'I am the Light of the world' (John 8:12) and 'I am the Resurrection and the life' (John 11:25) can also say 'I am a worm'. Like the first words of the psalm, we find ourselves once again on the edge of the most profound mystery.

Such shame

The shame that Jesus feels is magnified by the cacophony of voices that surround him as he hangs in agony. This was predicted a thousand years earlier in our psalm:

> *All who see me mock me;*
> *they hurl insults, shaking their heads.*
> *'He trusts in the Lord,' they say,*
> *'let the Lord rescue him.*
> *Let him deliver him,*
> *since he delights in him.'* (Verse 7–8)

Wicked people will shake their heads at Jesus in a gesture of derision. In particular, they will attack the foundation of his very existence – his relationship with his Father. Jesus often spoke of the intimacy he enjoyed with God. Just hours before the cross, he spoke to his Father in the most tender and affectionate terms:

> *Father, the hour has come. Glorify your Son, that your Son may glorify you … And now,*

> *Father, glorify me in your presence with the glory I had with you before the world began.* (John 17:1, 5)

That intimacy will soon be tested when Jesus descends into the darkness, but even before this happens the mockery of his relationship with the Father is predicted.

This mockery begins before the cross. The Jewish Sanhedrin condemn Jesus for predicting that they will see him, the Son of Man, seated at the right hand of God and coming on the clouds of glory (Mark 14:60–64). The guards mock him as a false prophet: 'Then some began to spit at him; they blindfolded him, struck him with their fists, and said, "Prophesy!" And the guards took him and beat him' (Mark 14:65). Time and again they kneel in mock homage and smash his face with their fists, asking the blindfolded prophet to predict who had thrown the punch.

Jesus is handed over to the Roman soldiers, and they mock his claims to kingship:

> *Then the governor's soldiers took Jesus into the Praetorium and gathered the whole company of soldiers around him. They stripped him and*

> *put a scarlet robe on him, and then twisted together a crown of thorns and set it on his head. They put a staff in his right hand. Then they knelt in front of him and mocked him. 'Hail, king of the Jews!' they said. They spat on him, and took the staff and struck him on the head again and again. After they had mocked him, they took off the robe and put his own clothes on him. Then they led him away to crucify him.* (Matthew 27:27–31)

The mockery continues as he hangs for three hours in the blazing sun:

> *Those who passed by hurled insults at him, shaking their heads and saying, 'You who are going to destroy the temple and build it in three days, save yourself! Come down from the cross, if you are the Son of God!' In the same way the chief priests, the teachers of the law and the elders mocked him. 'He saved others,' they said, 'but he can't save himself! He's the king of Israel! Let him come down now from the cross, and we will believe in him. He trusts in God. Let God rescue him now if he wants him, for he said, "I am the Son of*

> *God.'"' In the same way the rebels who were crucified with him also heaped insults on him.* (Matthew 27:39–44)

Notice that this strident scorn sweeps over Jesus from all directions – passers-by, religious leaders, soldiers and condemned criminals. Do they know that they are fulfilling prophecy? They mock Jesus because they want to; at the same time they are playing the part that God has ordained for them!

How could they be so cruel? When someone is close to death, we tend to cloak their final hours with quiet respect. Not so with Jesus. Before divine darkness silences his critics, Jesus is the subject of a constant stream of abuse. There are a few friendly faces, such as the women who faithfully follow him and his disciple John. One of the thieves will repent and recognise a beauty in Jesus which only faith can see. But for three hours Jesus' soul is lacerated by the words of wicked men. Imagine their scorn:

> *If you are really God's Son, as you claim, why have you been nailed to a cross? Why has God forsaken you? This is no way to treat*

> *your friends! Your whole mission is a sham! A Saviour who cannot save himself is no Saviour! You are a deluded blasphemer and you are getting what you deserve.*

Did Jesus feel the sting of their words? Of course he did! We have sometimes downplayed his humanity because we have wanted to defend his deity. We need to remember that he was both God and man – one person with two natures which are without confusion, change, division or separation. Words hurt! In Jesus' human nature, made vulnerable by the physical and psychological trauma of crucifixion, the temptation to doubt God's love and fear that his mission was a complete failure must have been real.

And this mockery of Jesus and his followers did not end at Calvary.

Indignity and humiliation

In 1857 Italian builders working on the Palatine Hill in the city of Rome unearthed the remains of a house dating back to Emperor Caligula, who ruled AD 37–41. On examination they discovered a piece of crude graffiti scrawled on one of the walls. It depicts a human-like figure nailed to a cross, but with the head of a donkey or mule. Next to the figure, which is clearly meant to represent Jesus, stands a young man, who is raising his hand in worship to the 'man' on the cross. Underneath is the inscription 'Alexamenos worships his God.'

The piece of graffiti is a sarcastic attack on the perceived absurdity of worshipping a God who ended up nailed to a cross. There is some speculation that pagans accused Christians of worshipping an ass, but the real stigma was the fact that Christians followed a God who could experience the shame of crucifixion.

In the first century there was no greater indignity.

Cicero argued that Roman citizens should not ever have to hear the word 'cross':

> *For not only the actual fact and endurance of all these things, but the bare possibility of being exposed to them, – the expectation, the mere mention of them even, – is unworthy of a Roman citizen and of a free man.*[2]

To understand the full horror of what Jesus endured for us, we have to recognise how shameful it was for him to experience the disgrace, humiliation and infamy of being crucified. Stripped naked and exposed to public display was a horrific prospect for anyone, but for a Jew it was even more appalling, as Jews prided themselves on their modesty. Jesus was stripped of his clothes and unprotected from the wicked glare and vile taunts of his enemies.

Made a curse

But there is an even greater dimension to the shame which Jesus experienced. Under the law of Moses a corpse was displayed after a public execution to indicate that the offender was under the curse of God:

> *If someone guilty of a capital offence is put to death and their body is exposed on a pole, you must not leave the body hanging on the pole overnight. Be sure to bury it that same day, because anyone who is hung on a pole is under God's curse. You must not desecrate the land the* L*ORD* *your God is giving you as an inheritance.* (Deuteronomy 21:22–23)

A crucified man was assumed to be an enemy of God, and was displayed in public as a warning to anyone who might fail to fear the Lord.

Paul picks up this common assumption in Galatians 3:13–14:

> *Christ redeemed us from the curse of the law by becoming a curse for us, for it is written: 'Cursed is everyone who is hung on a pole.' He redeemed us in order that the blessing given to Abraham might come to the Gentiles through Christ Jesus, so that by faith we might receive the promise of the Spirit.*

But notice how Paul turns the thinking on its head. Yes, the cross was a place where God's curse was fully displayed and his punishment of sin reached its fullest expression. However, the curse that Christ took upon himself was on our behalf. As one hymn so wonderfully puts it:

> *Bearing shame and scoffing rude,*
> *In my place condemned He stood;*
> *Sealed my pardon with His blood;*
> *Hallelujah! what a Saviour!*[3]

Strengthening his soul in the Lord

Yet, as tempting as it is to doubt God's loving care, Jesus does not fall into a pit of despair. Returning to Psalm 22, the psalmist confesses the reality of the shame he feels, but at the same time strengthens his soul by remembering God's paternal care:

> *Yet you brought me out of the womb;*
> *you made me trust in you, even at my mother's breast.*
> *From birth I was cast on you;*
> *from my mother's womb you have been my God.* (Verses 9–10)

Amid the maelstrom of hate and mockery, he remembers his earliest conscious memories of his Father's care. God has been with him from before his birth. God is not a casual acquaintance. He had known the Father's presence since infancy.

Jesus' first recorded words are at the age of twelve, when his parents have come to the temple searching for him. Jesus' response shocks them: '"Why were you searching for me?" he asked. "Didn't you know I had to be in my Father's house?"' (Luke 2:49). Jesus begins his mission under the smile of divine approval (Matthew 3:16–17) and, in spite of the horror of the cross, his last recorded words before death express confidence and faith in the Father's care: 'Jesus called out with a loud voice, "Father, into your hands I commit my spirit." When he had said this, he breathed his last' (Luke 23:46).

Jesus knows that his enemies are wrong. The cross is not a sign of divine disapproval; it is the Lord's will. The suffering is not accidental or meaningless. While the shame is real and terrible, it is part of God's purpose to save rebels. This is why Jesus did not come down from the cross. He was obeying the Father. He was saving sinners. He was fulfilling his mission. As has been observed:

> *To descend from the cross was not indeed a physical impossibility, but it was a moral and spiritual impossibility for the Messiah. If he did so, he would cease to be God's Christ, treading God's path of Messiahship; instead, he would become a mere human Christ, and such a Christ could never save the world. The*

> *only path by which to save others was to refuse to save himself.*[4]

Jesus deliberately humbled himself. He exchanged glory for Golgotha; the worship of heaven for the mockery of earth; the adoration of angels for the scorn of soldiers. He consciously and deliberately did this to save people like us. And he did so while we were still sinners – the kind of people who were mocking him.

I think of the testimony of a man converted in his sixties:

> *All my life I made fun of Christians. I made crude jokes about Jesus. I thought I was being clever. And then I got cancer. I was terrified of dying and I cried out for mercy. And he came to me and lifted me up. All my life I've kicked Jesus in the teeth – but when I needed him, he was there for me. All I want to do for the rest of my life is to tell people how brilliant he is.*

This short section in Psalm 22 ends with an appeal to God as the only one who can help:

Do not be far from me,
for trouble is near
and there is no one to help. (Verse 11)

Like the last prayer of Jesus on the cross, the picture is of a child falling asleep in the comforting embrace of a loving Father.

The early Christians knew that the cross was shameful – that proclaiming a crucified Messiah would be a major cause of misunderstanding and mockery. Yet they refused to back down. When Paul arrives in Corinth, he feels weak and is almost overcome with fear and trembling. He knows that, in this highly educated city, the idea of a crucified God will be treated with contempt and derision. Why not downplay it? Instead, Paul is adamant: 'For I resolved to know nothing while I was with you except Jesus Christ and him crucified' (1 Corinthians 2:2).

Why this resolution? The world may treat the cross as shameful, but Paul knows that in the cross God's wisdom is displayed and God's power is released:

Jews demand signs and Greeks look for wisdom, but we preach Christ crucified: a

> *stumbling block to Jews and foolishness to Gentiles, but to those whom God has called, both Jews and Greeks, Christ the power of God and the wisdom of God. For the foolishness of God is wiser than human wisdom, and the weakness of God is stronger than human strength.* (1 Corinthians 1:22–25)

Paul shared in the shame of Jesus and we are called to do likewise. It has always been so. Returning to the ancient graffiti mentioned earlier, next to the words 'Alexamenos worships his God', another hand had added 'Alexamenos is faithful'. Was this a follower of Jesus? Did they want to deny the blasphemy of the picture and at the same time affirm that faithfulness to Christ demands allegiance to the cross?

No one knows. But as believers we should never be ashamed of the cross. Jesus has transformed a place of shame into a place of glory. Like Paul we can confess, 'May I never boast except in the cross of our Lord Jesus Christ, through which the world has been crucified to me, and I to the world' (Galatians 6:14).

QUESTIONS

1. As he suffers, Jesus meditates on the intimacy of his relationship with his Father. How can this help us when we face mockery and derision because of our faith?
2. Read John 12:20–33. What do these verses teach us about Jesus' understanding of the cross?
3. Why might we be tempted to be ashamed of the cross today? How can we 'glory in the cross'?

4

I AM CRUCIFIED

12 *Many bulls surround me;*
strong bulls of Bashan encircle me.
13 *Roaring lions that tear their prey*
open their mouths wide against me.
14 *I am poured out like water,*
and all my bones are out of joint.
My heart has turned to wax;
it has melted within me.
15 *My mouth is dried up like a potsherd,*
and my tongue sticks to the roof of my mouth;
you lay me in the dust of death.

16 *Dogs surround me,*
a pack of villains encircles me;
they pierce my hands and my feet.

17 All my bones are on display;
people stare and gloat over me.
18 They divide my clothes among them
and cast lots for my garment.

19 But you, LORD, do not be far from me.
You are my strength; come quickly to help me.
20 Deliver me from the sword,
my precious life from the power of the dogs.
21 Rescue me from the mouth of the lions;
save me from the horns of the wild oxen.
(Psalm 22:12–21)

Jesus knew

In this section of the psalm, as we once again look forward to Good Friday, we stand amazed in the presence of Jesus the Nazarene as he dies in agony impaled on a Roman gibbet. But before we turn to the psalm, let's think for a few moments about crucifixion in the first century.

There were millions of slaves in the Roman Empire. How do you suppress revolt and ensure docile obedience? You use a form of execution which is both ferociously barbaric and public. Crucifixion fitted the bill perfectly.

Invented by the Babylonians, it was refined by the Persians. Alexander the Great brought crucifixion west where, from the third century BC, it was adopted by the Romans. They used crucifixion for five hundred years until Constantine abolished it in AD 337. It was often preceded by a scourging. Death itself was caused by a mixture of horrific factors including dehydration and asphyxia. Crucifixion was the ultimate deterrent.

Criminals were usually crucified in public places, especially near roads where passers-by could witness the cost of contesting the power of the Roman state. To press the matter home, the victim was guarded until death, and then the carcass was left on display for all to see. The Roman general Varus crucified 2,000 Jews in 4 BC, which means crucifixion would have been a common sight.

As such, it is most likely that, during his life, Jesus witnessed more than one example. From childhood he would have known about the horrors of crucifixion. As Jesus read verses 12–21 of our psalm, he could not have avoided the vivid description of crucifixion. Some of the descriptions are couched in the poetic language of metaphor, but others are clear and graphic.

The mystery of how Jesus possessed full deity and full humanity in one person is beyond human comprehension. How could he know all things and yet at the same time be able to learn things in the same way that we do? We can only wonder and marvel. But at some point, as Jesus read the prophecies of the Old Testament, he came to see that his mission would lead to death. And as he read Psalm 22, the full horror dawned on him that it would be death on a cross.

> *From that time on Jesus began to explain to his disciples that he must go to Jerusalem and suffer many things at the hands of the elders, the chief priests and the teachers of the law, and that he must be killed and on the third day be raised to life.* (Matthew 16:21)

Immediately after this prediction Jesus indicated precisely the mode of death he would suffer:

> *Then Jesus said to his disciples, 'Whoever wants to be my disciple must deny themselves*

> *and take up their cross and follow me'.* (Matthew 16:24)

Jesus knew.

How could they be so cruel?

William Wordsworth defines poetry as 'the spontaneous overflow of powerful feelings'.[1] David was a master of the art. As he describes the scene around the cross, he uses a series of powerful images to try to capture its horror.

He begins by painting a picture of the animalistic violence that would overwhelm Jesus:

> *Many bulls surround me;*
> *strong bulls of Bashan encircle me.*
> *Roaring lions that tear their prey*
> *open their mouths wide against me.*
> (Verses 12–13)

> *Dogs surround me,*
> *a pack of villains encircles me…* (Verse 16)

The victim on the cross feels as if he is being crushed by bulls, or mauled by lions, or torn by dogs. Bashan was a place of lush foliage that was famed for the size and strength of its bulls. Imagine being surrounded by a herd of violent creatures with nowhere to hide. Or imagine the climax of the hunt where, in a frenzy of blood, the dogs tear their quarry to pieces. The psalm is set to the tune 'The doe of the morning' – we know nothing about the tune, but perhaps David chose it to fit with the animal imagery.

The images are meant to shock us. They graphically portray the bloody violence which crucifixion involved. This is not a sanitised death. Forget the golden crucifixes studded with gems that are treasured by some churches. This is brutal and ferocious and vile.

The images also remind us of the animalistic cruelty of those who murdered the Messiah. Here we witness the assault of wicked men. Their actions are pitiless and inhuman. They pursue Jesus and corner him and tear him apart. As Matthew tells us:

Then he [Pilate] released Barabbas to them [the people]. But he had Jesus flogged and handed him over to be crucified.

Then the governor's soldiers took Jesus into the Praetorium and gathered the whole

> *company of soldiers round him. They stripped him and put a scarlet robe on him, and then twisted together a crown of thorns and set it on his head. They put a staff in his right hand. Then they knelt in front of him and mocked him. 'Hail, king of the Jews!' they said. They spat on him, and took the staff and struck him on the head again and again. After they had mocked him, they took off the robe and put his own clothes on him. Then they led him away to crucify him.* (Matthew 27:26–31)

How could they be so cruel?

The cross demonstrates the terrible wickedness of sin. It is a direct assault on deity. It is an attempt to remove divine constraints – a radical declaration of revolt against God. To mock Jesus, the soldiers blindfold him and then strike him in the face. Sin is like such a violent blow to the face of God – a direct and furious rejection of his authority. It is deliberate and high-handed defiance.

God becomes a man and what do humans do? They crucify him.

We confidently insist that we would never exhibit such cruelty. And yet, if we are honest, there are all kinds of wild beasts lurking in our hearts. If God were to remove his restraining hand, we would see that we are capable of all kinds of cruelty. The cross is a kind of mirror which reveals the dark things that lurk in our hearts. C.S. Lewis describes his growing self-knowledge in this way:

> *For the first time I examined myself with a seriously practical purpose. And there I found what appalled me; a zoo of lusts, a bedlam of ambitions, a nursery of fears, a harem of fondled hatreds. My name was legion.*[2]

'I am thirsty'

David also paints a picture of intense thirst.

> *I am poured out like water,*
> *and all my bones are out of joint.*
> *My heart has turned to wax;*
> *it has melted within me.*
> *My mouth is dried up like a potsherd,*
> *and my tongue sticks to the roof of*
> *my mouth;*
> *you lay me in the dust of death.*
> (Verses 14–15)

John begins his Gospel by telling us that Jesus is the source of life: 'In him was life, and that life was the light of all mankind' (John 1:4). Now Jesus is being poured out. He sees this life spilling from his veins like water cascading into the dirt. The strong Son of God sees his heart melted as in a raging furnace. At the height of his sufferings he will cry out, 'I am thirsty' (John 19:28). This is perhaps the most human of all the cries from the cross. But, once again, what a mystery. The Creator of the universe is thirsty! The one who rules and reigns at the Father's right hand gasps for a drink! The eternal Son of God yearns for the touch of a few drops of water!

Of course these images point to the very real physicality of death. Death is dry. I remember moistening my dad's lips during the last hours of his life. In Jesus' case it is not surprising that he feels thirst. He has lost so much blood and has been exposed to the elements as he hangs from this cruel Roman gibbet. This is a clear prelude to death.

But is there more here? Is the thirst of his body matched by the thirst of his soul? For three hours he has been in the darkness. As we have seen, darkness is a symbol of judgement.

Hell is a place of outer darkness where there is 'weeping and gnashing of teeth' (Matthew 8:12). But another common image of God's wrath against sin is the fire which burns without destroying. Our God is 'a consuming fire' (Hebrews 12:29). In hell the unrepentant rich man cries out:

> *Father Abraham, have pity on me and send Lazarus to dip the tip of his finger in water and cool my tongue, because I am in agony in this fire'*. (Luke 16:24)

This is another indication of the profound suffering the Saviour endures as he takes responsibility for our sins and bears the full force of God's fierce anger in our place. As Charles Wesley's hymn declares:

> *For what you have done His blood must atone:*
> *The Father hath punished for you His dear Son.*
> *The Lord, in the day of His anger, did lay*
> *Your sins on the Lamb, and He bore them away.*[3]

At the same time, this revelation of the full humanity of Jesus is a wonderful comfort for us.

When we suffer or when we weep or when our hearts are filled with grief, we know that we have a Saviour and friend who feels our weaknesses. He whispers in our ears:

> *Come to me, all you who are weary and burdened, and I will give you rest. Take my yoke upon you and learn from me, for I am gentle and humble in heart, and you will find rest for your souls. For my yoke is easy and my burden is light.* (Matthew 11:28–30)

History foretold

Beyond the metaphors, this section of the psalm contains specific predictions of the crucifixion:

> *... they pierce my hands and my feet.*
> *All my bones are on display;*
> *people stare and gloat over me.*
> *They divide my clothes among them*
> *and cast lots for my garment.* (Verses 16–18)

How do we explain this if it is not the result of divine foreknowledge? The Bible is a supernatural book. What the Old Testament predicted was embodied in the life and death of Jesus. Could he have deliberately staged some events in his life to coincide with what the Bible had predicted? Was he merely an actor following a script? No! You cannot stage the place of your birth (Matthew 2:1–6) or the mode of your death! You cannot cause Roman soldiers to cast lots for your garments (John 19:23–24).

Another prophetic example is that when the soldiers come to break Jesus' legs in order to hasten his death, they find that he has already died and so his bones remain intact. Referring to Psalm 34:19–20 and Zechariah 12:10, John tells us:

> *These things happened so that the scripture would be fulfilled: 'Not one of his bones will be broken,' and, as another scripture says, 'They will look on the one they have pierced'.* (John 19:36–37)

That is not something that can be staged either!

Someone has estimated that, in his life and death, Jesus fulfilled 300 prophecies. We can trust the Bible because it bears the stamp of divine authenticity.

'... you lay me in the dust of death'

Psalm 22 may reflect some of David's experiences, but as we have seen, it breaks the boundaries and passes way beyond anything that happened in his life. This is true in so many ways, but quite specifically the psalm ends in the death of the victim. He is laid in the dust of death.

People have found many ways to describe and perhaps anaesthetise death, but this simple phrase is both graphic and profound. What is death? Human beings have a body and a soul. Both are essential to what we are – they are what make us human. They belong together. Death occurs at that moment when the body and the soul separate (Ecclesiastes 12:6–7).

The crucifixion of Jesus ends in his death:

> *It was now about noon, and darkness came over the whole land until three in the afternoon, for the sun stopped shining. And the curtain of the temple was torn in two. Jesus called out with a loud voice, 'Father, into your hands I commit my spirit.' When he had said this, he breathed his last.* (Luke 23:44–46)

As Jesus deliberately 'gave up his spirit' (Matthew 27:50; John 19:30), his last breath carried this final prayer. These words of Jesus echo the prayers of a Jewish child, based on Psalm 31, as they lay down to sleep at night. They express the child's confidence in the Father's care. The darkness is over. Here, in Jesus' final prayer, we see that fellowship with the Father is restored. He looks beyond the cross to the glory of the resurrection. And even as he dies, Jesus may be remembering Psalm 22, which expresses the same confident trust in deliverance:

> *But you, Lord, do not be far from me.*
> *You are my strength; come quickly to help me.*
> *Deliver me from the sword,*
> *my precious life from the power of the dogs.*
> *Rescue me from the mouth of the lions;*
> *save me from the horns of the wild oxen.*
> (Verses 19–21)

More than history

But there is more to this story than history. We can be confident that what the four Gospels describe really happened in a particular place and at a particular moment in time. Yet it is more than the tragic death of a good man. These events were predicted in advance and wrapped around with explanation afterwards. The cross unlocks a treasury of endless blessings. Jesus dies to conquer Satan and bring about the possibility of a new creation. He dies to leave us an example of sacrificial love. He demonstrates beyond any possible doubt that the Father loves us and is willing to pay the ultimate price to save us.

At the heart of this event is what the theologians call 'penal substitutionary atonement'. For those of us who may be slightly overawed by theology, it is worth stretching our minds a little. This glorious doctrine is the non-negotiable heart of the Christian gospel. Lose it and we lose everything. This is the anchor which secures every other blessing – forgiveness, reconciliation with God, assurance of salvation, holiness, hope and heaven.

So what is penal substitutionary atonement? Theologians use the word 'penal' because it relates to the execution of punishment for the violation of a law. The law breaker suffers a penalty for his crime. On the cross Jesus is not just leaving us an example; he is being punished. He is being treated as a criminal and is experiencing the full weight of the punishment that sin deserves. Hell is a place of darkness, separation and burning wrath. On the cross Jesus experiences all these things in the most profound way.

It is 'substitutionary' because Jesus is bearing this judgement not for his own sins but for ours. He had no debt to pay because he had not broken any law. He was totally innocent and utterly holy. But he takes responsibility for the sins of the world. He carries the punishment others deserve – David's adultery, Peter's denial, Paul's persecution of the church and the just retribution due to countless others like you and me.

It is 'atonement' because God, the holy Judge, is satisfied. He is content that the full price has been paid. On this basis, without compromising his holiness and justice, he delights to welcome repentant sinners back into fellowship with himself. This is not a vindictive God punishing an innocent Jesus. All three members of the Trinity are offended by our sin. All three are motivated by sacrificial love, and are determined to deal with sin and accomplish salvation. The one nailed to the cross is the sin-hating, salvation-winning God. And the same is true of the Father who so loved the world that he gave the darling of his heart to redeem sinners.

For the first Christians the cross was a place of splendid, agonising, blood-soaked, passion-driven glory.

The dying thief witnesses the horror of crucifixion firsthand. But as he looks at Jesus, he sees something more than crucifixion. He sees beauty in ugliness; he sees majesty in ruin; he sees glory in shame; he sees victory in defeat; he sees royalty in rejection; he sees life in death.

What do you see today?

QUESTIONS

1. Jesus knew that he would be crucified. What does that teach us about him? How should we respond?
2. 'The cross is a kind of mirror which reveals the dark things that lurk in our hearts.' Why is it good for us to look in this mirror?
3. Consider again the definition of penal substitutionary atonement. Why is

this truth so important? What are the implications for our everyday life and for our Christian witness?

Part 2

EASTER SUNDAY ANNOUNCED

The first part of Psalm 22 takes us into the darkness and ends with an earnest cry for salvation. The psalmist has reached the bottom of a horrible pit, but he is quietly confident that the God he has always trusted will rescue him.

In the second half of the psalm, God answers his cry for help. As we have seen, the psalm moves beyond David's experience, and in these verses we contemplate resurrection morning and the conquest of the grave. In place of grief and tears we find exultation and jubilation. The victorious Saviour invites us to revel in his triumph and all that it has accomplished. More than that, he calls us to announce his victory to the nations.

The triumph of the Crucified is the subject of the next two chapters:

1. Celebration: Jesus is risen (verses 22–26).
2. Proclamation: Jesus is Lord (verses 27–31).

5

CELEBRATION: JESUS IS RISEN

22 *I will declare your name to my people;*
in the assembly I will praise you.
23 *You who fear the LORD, praise him!*
All you descendants of Jacob, honour him!
Revere him, all you descendants of Israel!
24 *For he has not despised or scorned*
the suffering of the afflicted one;
he has not hidden his face from him
but has listened to his cry for help.
25 *From you comes the theme of my praise in the great assembly;*
before those who fear you I will fulfil my vows.
26 *The poor will eat and be satisfied;*
those who seek the LORD will praise him –
may your hearts live for ever! (Psalm 22:22–26)

I will declare

Meditating on Psalm 22, Jesus knows that he was born to die. He will be laid in the 'dust of death' (verse 15).

But that is not all Jesus knows. He also knows that beyond the grave will be the resurrection. So Jesus echoes David's words, asking his Father to rescue him (verse 21) and then immediately announcing his confidence that his Father will answer:

> *I will declare your name to my people;*
> *in the assembly I will praise you ...*
> *For he has not despised or scorned*
> *the suffering of the afflicted one;*
> *he has not hidden his face from him*
> *but has listened to his cry for help.*
> (Verses 22, 24)

Jesus' whole life is animated by the promises of Scripture. He is convinced that the cross is not the end. Jesus is the 'pioneer and perfecter of faith. For the joy that was set before him he endured the cross, scorning its shame, and sat down at the right hand of the throne of God' (Hebrews 12:2).

His is a model of true faith. It's what true faith looks like. This faith springs from trust in God's Word and flows into courageous abandon to God's purposes.

Jesus knows that he will rise because he has read the prophecies in Psalm 22. He deliberately follows the path the Father had set for him. After committing his spirit into his Father's hands, he breathes his last (Luke 23:46). His spirit goes to be with his Father in Paradise (Luke 23:43) while his body rests in Joseph's tomb (Luke 23:50–54).

Three day later, his spirit is reunited with his body – which, after the resurrection, has been totally transformed into a glorious body. His heart begins to beat. His eyelids flutter. His lungs fill with breath. Up from the grave he arises with a mighty triumph over his foes!

There is no other explanation

If you studied theology at Cambridge University in the 1970s, you almost certainly attended the lectures of Charlie Moule. Charles Francis Digby Moule was the Lady Margaret's Professor of Divinity at the university. Born of missionary parents in Hangzhou, China, he was the great-nephew of Handley Moule, the godly Bishop of

Durham. A humble, prayerful man, Charlie had a profound faith. Like his great-uncle, he became known affectionately as 'Holy Mouley'.

As a second-year undergraduate, I attended his lectures on 'New Testament Theology and Ethics'. (I still have the notes forty-five years later!) A fairly naïve Bible-believing Christian, I had been struggling with the liberal theology that many of my teachers espoused. Did any of them share my simple faith? Then I attended Charlie Moule's lectures. Amazingly he invited us to pray before he started – unheard of in the theology faculty! And then he began his first lecture. I will never forget his opening words:

> *Ladies and gentlemen, we are about to study the great theme of New Testament Theology and Ethics. If Jesus Christ had not risen from the dead, there would be no New Testament Theology and Ethics. There would be no New Testament. There would be no church. But Christ is risen. There is no other explanation. Hallelujah!*

I didn't have the courage to echo his hallelujah, but my heart leapt!

Many infallible proofs

My professor was right. The Christian church has the resurrection written all over it. The empty tomb and the risen Saviour are the only explanations of the birth and growth of the early church. Christianity stands or falls on this foundation, and the foundation is solid and sure. The resurrection of Christ is not a lovely story with symbolic meaning. It is not a parable or an allegory or an inspiring legend. It is physical and datable and real.

The fact of the resurrection transforms the disciples and is the heart of their message. Read through the sermons in Acts. They constantly proclaim Jesus' cross and resurrection. They really are one-trick ponies! Think of Peter's Pentecost sermon. He boldly proclaims:

> *Fellow Israelites, listen to this: Jesus of Nazareth was a man accredited by God to you by miracles, wonders and signs, which God did among you through him, as you yourselves know. This man was handed over to you by God's deliberate plan and foreknowledge; and you, with the help of wicked men, put*

> *him to death by nailing him to the cross. But God raised him from the dead, freeing him from the agony of death, because it was impossible for death to keep its hold on him.* (Acts 2:22–24)

To summarise what Peter is saying to the crowd: Jesus was a real man – you know it! Jesus died on the cross – you did it! Jesus rose from the dead – we saw it!

Peter then appeals to two lines of evidence to support his case. There is of course the eyewitness testimony of the apostles. They had met with Jesus for forty days after his resurrection, during which he had proved that he was alive by 'many convincing proofs' (Acts 1:3). They were willing to die rather than deny the evidence of their own eyes.

But Peter then goes on to show that the resurrection was predicted by the Old Testament prophets. He quotes Psalms 16:8–11 and 110:1 to clinch his case (see Acts 2:25–28 and 34–35). During the forty days that the risen Jesus had spent teaching his disciples, the Old Testament had begun to unlock its treasures:

> *Then he opened their minds so they could understand the Scriptures. He told them, 'This is what is written: the Messiah will suffer and rise from the dead on the third day, and repentance for the forgiveness of sins will be preached in his name to all nations, beginning at Jerusalem. You are witnesses of these things'.* (Luke 24:45–48)

It's highly likely that part of the Lord's curriculum would have included Psalm 22!

Easter Sunday evening

What does Jesus do after his resurrection? He goes to comfort his disciples and declare that death has been conquered. He again echoes the words of Psalm 22: 'I will declare your name to my people; in the assembly I will praise you' (verse 22).

John tells us that Jesus' first resurrection appearance is to Mary Magdalene. She clearly wants to reach out and grip him because Jesus says:

> *Do not hold on to me, for I have not yet ascended to the Father. Go instead to my*

> *brothers and tell them, 'I am ascending to my Father and your Father, to my God and your God.'* (John 20:17)

She obeys the Lord. John, the eyewitness, continues:

> *On the evening of that first day of the week, when the disciples were together, with the doors locked for fear of the Jewish leaders, Jesus came and stood among them and said, 'Peace be with you!' After he said this, he showed them his hands and side. The disciples were overjoyed when they saw the Lord.* (John 20:19–20)

Jesus is fulfilling the predictions of Psalm 22 literally as he stands before his brothers and sisters and declares that the Father has raised him from the dead.

Luke describes the same event:

> *While they were still talking about this, Jesus himself stood among them and said to them, 'Peace be with you.'*

They were startled and frightened, thinking they saw a ghost. He said to them, 'Why are you troubled, and why do doubts rise in your minds? Look at my hands and my feet. It is I myself! Touch me and see; a ghost does not have flesh and bones, as you see I have.'

When he had said this, he showed them his hands and feet. And while they still did not believe it because of joy and amazement, he asked them, 'Do you have anything here to eat?' They gave him a piece of broiled fish, and he took it and ate it in their presence.

He said to them, 'This is what I told you while I was still with you: everything must be fulfilled that is written about me in the Law of Moses, the Prophets and the Psalms'. (Luke 24:36–44)

Joyful praise

The disciples react with mixed emotions. They are startled and afraid, but Jesus tenderly speaks peace into their troubled hearts. Jesus has every right to reprimand them for their lack of courage. But instead of scolding them, Jesus' first words are, 'Peace be with you'!

Their fear is turned into faith, and their faith overflows in joy and amazement. This joy will result in spontaneous praise and confident proclamation.

And this is exactly what Psalm 22 predicted. The resurrection of Jesus results in a threefold invitation to celebration:

> *You who fear the Lord, praise him!*
> *All you descendants of Jacob, honour him!*
> *Revere him, all you descendants of Israel!*
> (Verse 23)

Derek Kidner calls these verses, 'The spread of joy'.[1] The disciples are all descendants of Jacob or Israel – they are God-fearing Jews. The message of the resurrection comes first to them. But this message is for all people (Matthew 28:18–20; Acts 1:8). The only appropriate response is universal worship.

As Christians, we now celebrate the fact that God heard Jesus' prayer and raised him from the grave. Jesus himself testifies the truth of Psalm 22:

For he has not despised or scorned
the suffering of the afflicted one;
he has not hidden his face from him
but has listened to his cry for help. (Verse 24)

How can we not be joyful in the face of the resurrection! But sadly this is often not the case, perhaps because we have the wrong idea about joy. The Bible describes the balanced Christian life using the analogy of fruit (Galatians 5:22–23). As God's Spirit lives within us, he manifests the life of Christ through us. This consists of one fruit which is displayed with nine indispensable facets. And number two on the list is joy, making joy non-negotiable. A joyless Christian is a contradiction in terms.

So what is joy? Some people are temperamentally jolly. It's not that. Nor is it circumstantial. We can have tears in our eyes and joy in our hearts. In the Bible, Christian joy flows from Christian truth. It is a deep-seated confidence in God and his promises. It is the assurance that in the end all things will be well.

And it is the resurrection of Christ which is the solid and immovable foundation of this joy!

The apostles couldn't stop talking about it! Even when they were threatened and beaten, they still could not stop:

> *They [the Jewish council] called the apostles in and had them flogged. Then they ordered them not to speak in the name of Jesus, and let them go.*
>
> *The apostles left the Sanhedrin, rejoicing because they had been counted worthy of suffering disgrace for the Name. Day after day, in the temple courts and from house to house, they never stopped teaching and proclaiming the good news that Jesus is the Messiah.* (Acts 5:40–42)

What turns flogging and disgrace into joy and courageous proclamation? The resurrection of Jesus!

I remember hearing a well-known preacher speaking on this subject. He described visiting a young man in a hospice. The man was terminally ill and the end was only a few weeks away. The sense of grief was real, but the overwhelming emotion was one of quiet confidence and anticipation.

The young man was insistent that they go through the order of service for the funeral: 'I want you to preach the gospel and I want it to be a time of celebration! Tell people not to wear black. I will be with the King.'

As he was leaving, one of the senior nurses asked to speak to the pastor. 'I'm really worried about that young man. He is dying but he doesn't seem to know it. He doesn't seem afraid or depressed in the least.'

The pastor assured her that he was fully aware of his situation and that they had been discussing funeral arrangements that morning.

The nurse was nonplussed:

> *It doesn't make any sense to me. I have not come across that kind of response before. All I can say is if he really does know that he is dying, then his response is unsuitably joyful!*

We can be 'unsuitably joyful' in the face of death because Christ is risen!

Welcome to the banquet

This joy is, of course, the great theme of the second half of Psalm 22. The contrast between the wretchedness of the first half and the overwhelming joy of the second half is obvious. It reminds us of the Gospels where the darkness of Good Friday is dispelled by the invincible light of Easter Sunday. It is the resurrection which makes all the difference. With the resurrection, the tectonic plates begin to shift. Everything is different now!

C.S. Lewis expresses it so well:

> *The New Testament writers speak as if Christ's achievement in rising from the dead was the first event of its kind in the whole history of the universe. He is the 'first fruits,' 'the pioneer of life.' He has forced open a door that has been locked since the death of the first man. He has met, fought, and beaten the King of Death. Everything is different because He has done so.*[2]

The proclamation of praise culminates in the description of a banquet in Psalm 22:

> *From you comes the theme of my praise in the great assembly;*
> *before those who fear you I will fulfil my vows.*
> *The poor will eat and be satisfied;*

> *those who seek the* Lord *will praise him –*
> *may your hearts live for ever!* (Verses 25–26)

Likewise, Jesus' prayer for deliverance from the grave has been granted and he invites his people to share in a feast of celebration. They must not keep their happiness to themselves but share it with everyone – even 'the poor will eat and be satisfied'.

Jesus dedicated himself to fulfilling the Father's plan. This involved dying for our sins and rising for our justification. He vowed to obey his Father and to drink from the cup which the Father gave him. Now that vow is fulfilled. The Father has heard his prayer and has raised him from the dead, highly exalting him (Philippians 2:9–11). It's time to feast – and Jesus invites us to join in the celebration!

Whenever we sit at the Lord's table, we take part in that feast. It is the solemn commemoration of his death. When we share bread and wine together, God speaks of his unchanging love towards us. But there is more than that. It is the table of the Lord because the Lord himself is there. In the words of Spurgeon's great hymn, 'amidst us our beloved stands'. The risen Lord reminds us that he is alive and we can feast at his table:

What generous food, what sweet accord,
when at his table sits the Lord!
How fine the bread, how rich the wine,
when Jesus calls his guests to dine!'[3]

Because Jesus is alive, we will one day share in the feast of heaven.

It was partly the joyful anticipation of feasting with his disciples which enabled Christ to endure the cross. He is not ashamed to call us brothers and sisters. Because he is alive, he will bring us safely to glory (Hebrews 2:10–18). The book of Revelation paints a beautiful picture of this:

Then I heard what sounded like a great multitude, like the roar of rushing waters and like loud peals of thunder, shouting:

Hallelujah!
    For our Lord God Almighty reigns.
Let us rejoice and be glad
    and give him glory!
For the wedding of the Lamb has come,

and his bride has made herself ready.
Fine linen, bright and clean,
was given her to wear. (Revelation 19:6–8)

This is our hope and expectation. The church, his bride, will one day feast in his presence. In the words of Charlie Moule, 'Christ is risen. There is no other explanation. Hallelujah!'

QUESTIONS

1. Read Hebrews 12:1–13. The author uses the example of Jesus' faith to inspire us. How does he apply this?
2. Read the accounts of Jesus' first resurrection appearance to the disciples in John 20:19–23 and Luke 24:36–49. What is the evidence that Jesus was not a ghost or that the disciples were not hallucinating?
3. Make a list of the blessings which flow from the resurrection. How should we respond?

6

PROCLAMATION: JESUS IS LORD

[27] *All the ends of the earth*
will remember and turn to the L*ORD*,
and all the families of the nations
will bow down before him,
[28] *for dominion belongs to the* L*ORD*
and he rules over the nations.
[29] *All the rich of the earth will feast and worship;*
all who go down to the dust will
kneel before him –
those who cannot keep themselves alive.
[30] *Posterity will serve him;*
future generations will be told about the Lord.
[31] *They will proclaim his righteousness,*
declaring to a people yet unborn:
He has done it! (Psalm 22:27–31)

The goal of mission

The theme of the last section of Psalm 22, as it once more directs us to Jesus' death and resurrection, is the mission of Christ and his church which flows from these realities.

Jesus has proclaimed his victory to his brothers (verse 22). Now he announces the Father's name to the nations so that they will turn to God:

> *All the ends of the earth*
> *will remember and turn to the Lord,*
> *and all the families of the nations*
> *will bow down before him,*
> *for dominion belongs to the Lord*
> *and he rules over the nations.* (Verses 27–28)

Jesus' suffering was not pointless. Because of his sacrifice, people all over the world will return to their Creator and worship him. Notice the threefold description of the response of the nations.

First, *they will remember*. The world has forgotten its Creator. People live in God's world without any thought of him. The evidence for God's existence is seen everywhere, but we supress it and choose to forget God's authority and majesty. Sitting in a pigsty of our own making, we forget the Father's house. But the proclamation of Christ's victory will cause us to come to our senses (Luke 15:17).

Second, *they will turn to the Lord*. This is a description of true repentance. It is more than a change of mind or sorrow for sin. It is a deliberate turning from sin to God. When Paul preached Christ's cross and resurrection to the pagans in Thessalonica, they:

> *... turned to God from idols to serve the living and true God, and to wait for his Son from heaven, whom he raised from the dead – Jesus, who rescues us from the coming wrath.* (1 Thessalonians 1:9–10)

Third, *they will bow down*. Repentant hearts become worshipping hearts. The nations come to acknowledge that the Lord reigns and that Christ will have a universal dominion, and they begin to give him the worship which he deserves. Indeed, this is the defining purpose of mission. John Piper puts it like this:

> *The goal of missions is the gladness of the peoples in the greatness of God. 'The* LORD *reigns, let the earth rejoice; let the many coastlands be glad!'* (Psalm 97:1). *'Let the peoples praise you, O God; let all the peoples praise you! Let the nations be glad and sing for joy!'* (Psalm 67:3–4) ... *Missions begins and ends in worship.*[1]

On the first Easter Sunday when the Lord appears to his disciples, guilt and fear become joy and celebration. It is out of this explosion of joy that Jesus sends them to the nations to proclaim that he is alive:

> *Again Jesus said, 'Peace be with you! As the Father has sent me, I am sending you.' And with that he breathed on them and said, 'Receive the Holy Spirit. If you forgive anyone's sins, their sins are forgiven; if you do not forgive them, they are not forgiven'.* (John 20:21–23)

The scope of mission is worldwide, and the power for mission is the gift of the Spirit. But notice that mission flows out of joy. What was foretold in Psalm 22 has now happened, just as it said it would, and cannot be suppressed! As a result, the nations will worship God and serve Christ as their King. As Lesslie Newbigin writes, *'Mission is an acted out doxology. That is its deepest secret. Its purpose is that God may be glorified.'*[2]

The glory of God is the passion of Jesus. It should be ours too. We are to be part of this mission as we spend our lives and our resources so that God's name will be honoured among the nations.

Here comes the bride

Elsewhere in the New Testament, Jesus is pictured as the Bridegroom who dies to rescue his beloved bride.

What is your favourite moment in a wedding ceremony? You know the sequence. The bridal party arrives. The organist begins to play the bridal march. Everyone stands. All eyes turn to the bride as, wreathed in smiles, she makes her way forward.

Everyone looks at the bride – except me! I have already welcomed her in the foyer. I have tipped the wink to the groom so that he knows that it is time to stand and welcome his bride. He, along with everyone else in the church, looks at her. But I look at him!

Most grooms are fairly nervous, but the vision of their gorgeous wife-to-be usually dispels the nerves – if only for a moment. I love to see that mixture of love, adoration and genuine amazement: 'I knew she was beautiful … but wow!'

All brides are beautiful on their wedding day and all grooms are amazed – at least in theory!

Now think about the church, because that should not be far from our minds when we attend a wedding. She is Christ's bride. He died for her and is preparing a place for her. She is his reward and his delight. She is beautiful in his eyes:

> *Christ loved the church and gave himself up for her to make her holy, cleansing her by the washing with water through the word, and to present her to himself as a radiant church, without stain or wrinkle or any other blemish, but holy and blameless.* (Ephesians 5:25–27)

The church may not look like that now, but when Christ returns, she will be 'without stain or wrinkle'. And he will be satisfied![3]

Just hours before the cross, Jesus prays for his church. He is about to descend into a volcano of pain and anguish. He pauses at the edge and prays. In the most intimate terms he remembers the glory he shared with the Father before the creation of the world. He then prays for his church, like a champion who has won a great victory and now claims his reward:

> *I have revealed you to those whom you gave me out of the world. They were yours; you gave them to me and they have obeyed your word.* (John 17:6)

What kept Jesus on target? What sustained him as he experienced the appalling sufferings described in Psalm 22? How could he endure the cross? It was 'for the joy that was set before him' (Hebrews 12:2) – and a great part of that joy was the delight he would have at the wedding supper of the Lamb, when his bride would be presented to him.

Like a mighty warrior rescuing his people from deadly danger, so Christ will rejoice as he rescues his church. The bridegroom has shed his blood to redeem his bride.

All nations

We may wonder about the exact scope of Jesus' mission. Again Psalm 22 gives us the answer.

This good news is to be proclaimed to the ends of the earth so that 'all the families of the nations will bow down before him', the Lord (verse 27). He 'rules over the nations' and they will acknowledge his dominion (verse 28).

This is one of the great themes of the psalms:

Shout for joy to God, all the earth!
Sing the glory of his name;
make his praise glorious.
Say to God, 'How awesome are your deeds!
So great is your power
that your enemies cringe before you.
All the earth bows down to you;
they sing praise to you,
they sing the praises of your name.'
(Psalm 66:1–4)

John glimpses this future reality in the book of Revelation:

> *After this I looked, and there before me was a great multitude that no one could count, from every nation, tribe, people and language, standing before the throne and before the Lamb. They were wearing white robes and were holding palm branches in their hands.* (Revelation 7:9)

A couple of years ago I was at a large conference. During the course of the week I met Christians from Bulgaria, Romania, Germany, Italy, France, USA, Canada, Sudan, South Africa, Brazil, Jamaica, India, China, Japan and South Korea. I even met a couple from Birmingham!

On the last night, at the end of the service, the person leading pronounced the benediction. There was silence for a few moments, then suddenly a single voice began to sing, 'There is a Redeemer; Jesus God's own Son …' Within seconds he was joined by 3,000 voices. It was one of those spine-tingling moments. Afterwards I reflected that this must be a little like what will happen in heaven when people from all nations, including the ones named above, join in the worship of God and of the Lamb! This is another image we see in the book of Revelation:

And they sang a new song, saying:

'You are worthy to take the scroll
and to open its seals,
because you were slain,
and with your blood you purchased for God
persons from every tribe and language and
people and nation.
You have made them to be a kingdom and priests
to serve our God,
and they will reign on the earth.'

Then I looked and heard the voice of many angels, numbering thousands upon thousands, and ten thousand times ten thousand. They encircled the throne and the living creatures and the elders. In a loud voice they were saying:

'Worthy is the Lamb, who was slain,
to receive power and wealth and
wisdom and strength
and honour and glory and praise!'
Then I heard every creature in heaven and on earth and under the earth and on the sea, and all that is in them, saying:

'To him who sits on the throne and to the Lamb
be praise and honour and glory and power,
for ever and ever!'

The four living creatures said, 'Amen,' and the elders fell down and worshipped.
(Revelation 5:9–14)

All conditions

But, returning to our psalm, we see that heaven is not just for all nations. It is also for all types of people:

The poor will eat and be satisfied;
those who seek the Lord will praise him –
may your hearts live for ever! (Verse 26)

All the rich of the earth will feast and worship;
all who go down to the dust will
kneel before him –
those who cannot keep themselves alive.
(Verse 29)

The salvation that Jesus secures is compared to a banquet – and everyone is welcome! The 'poor' will eat their fill and be satisfied. The word used to describe these people could mean 'meek' or 'humble' or 'lowly'. They seek Christ and, finding him, they find eternal satisfaction.

Is this a description of an economic or a spiritual condition? Jesus commends those who are 'poor in spirit' (Matthew 5:3), describing those who acknowledge their spiritual bankruptcy and cast themselves on God's grace. Think of the tax collector in the temple who beats his breast and cries out, 'God, have mercy on me, a sinner' (Luke 18:13).

Spurgeon takes it this way:

> *The spiritually poor find a feast in Jesus, they feed upon him to the satisfaction of their hearts, they were famished until he gave himself for them but now they are filled with royal dainties.*[4]

Or maybe the psalmist is thinking of the 'poor of the land', those who are destitute. Jesus acknowledged that there would always be those who were economically disadvantaged (Mark 14:7). But a lack of worldly goods does not exclude anyone from the gospel banquet.

At the same time, in verse 29 of the psalm, we see that the banquet will also feature some who were among 'the rich of the earth'. Jesus warns that riches are dangerous. One of his parables is about a rich man who feasted in life with no thought of the poor man at his door. The outcome is that the rich man is excluded from the banquet at Abraham's bosom (Luke 16:19–31). But there is no inverted snobbery in the Bible. It may be difficult for the rich man to enter the kingdom of heaven, but with God all things are possible (Matthew 19:23–26)!

Psalm 22 also speaks of those who 'go down to the dust' and who 'cannot keep themselves alive' (verse 29). They too will one day kneel in worship. The New Testament links the resurrection of Christ with the resurrection of his people – he is the firstfruits of those who have fallen asleep (1 Corinthians 15:20–22).

The gospel crosses all barriers of class, race, gender and age. Every kind of person is invited to the feast. Think of the way in which Jesus extends the invitation in his parables (Luke 14:15–24). Through his death he destroys all human barriers:

> *For he himself is our peace, who has made the two groups one and has destroyed the barrier, the dividing wall of hostility, by setting aside in his flesh the law with its commands and regulations. His purpose was to create in himself one new humanity out of the two, thus making peace, and in one body to reconcile both of them to God through the cross, by which he put to death their hostility. He came and preached peace to you who were far away and peace to those who were near.* (Ephesians 2:14–17)

My friend Glenn grew up in a Fundamentalist church in Mississippi in the 1970s. His church was very strong on the authority of the Authorised Version of the Bible and railed against the 'wishy-washy liberals' who didn't believe everything literally:

> *We knew we were right and everyone else was wrong. But I will never forget Sunday mornings. Two deacons would stand at the doors. They were both big men – ex-football players. And if a person of colour came near our church, they would be very firmly told,*

> *'This church is not for you! Your church is up the road.'*

How can you say that you believe the Bible and yet be so wrong in your application? Jesus broke down all humanly constructed barriers and invited everyone to come to him.

Trusting what Jesus did on the cross is the only way to be right with God. Everyone is welcome. That includes you. Have you accepted the invitation yet?

All time

Psalm 22 has already declared that the gospel is for all nations and for all types of people, but it is also for all time:

> *Posterity will serve him;*
> *future generations will be told about the Lord.*
> *They will proclaim his righteousness,*
> *declaring to a people yet unborn:*
> *He has done it!* (Verses 30–31)

God's kingdom will never fail. His righteousness, so dearly bought, will be proclaimed to 'future generations' and to 'people yet unborn'. The gospel is only ever one generation away from extinction. The faith of their parents will not save anyone. It is the task of every generation to pass on the gospel baton, praying for the genuine conversion of those who hear. This is a huge task.

James Johnson writes:

> *When will the work be done? As long as there are children in the world, our job is not complete. About a quarter of the world's population is under fifteen years of age – 1.8 billion young people. Of these, roughly 80 percent, or 1.4 billion, are growing up where they will never hear the gospel. Who will tell this new generation about God who raised Jesus Christ?*[5]

This should be a great challenge, but it should not cause us anxiety. God has promised an inheritance to Jesus: his bride, the church. He will not fail to grant him the reward he deserves. And Jesus will be satisfied.

Come and join the celebration

This last section of Psalm 22 is a picture of Jesus inviting us to come to him and feast at his table.

The invitation is universal. We feast at his table with Christ now, but this is only a pale reflection of the glory which is to be.

Jesus will be satisfied when he sees his bride. He will lead her into the marriage supper of the Lamb. Here she will feast with him for ever.

And what he offers is nothing less than total spiritual satisfaction. Jonathan Edwards, the great American theologian, expresses it like this:

> *God is the highest good of the reasonable creature, and the enjoyment of him is the only happiness with which our souls can be satisfied ... Fathers, mothers, husbands, wives, children or the company of earthly friends, are but shadows. But the enjoyment of God is the substance. These are but the scattered beams, but God is the sun. These are but the streams, but God is the fountain. These are but the drops, but God is the ocean.*[6]

Here is the heart of the gospel: through his death and resurrection, Jesus offers us an intimate and totally satisfying relationship with God. What is offered in the gospel is God himself! As he regularly affirms in the covenant blessings of the Old Testament, 'I will be your God, and you will be my people' (Exodus 6:7; Jeremiah 31:33; Hebrews 8:10; Revelation 21:3).

We will then be taken up with him. We will only have eyes for him.

In the words of a great old hymn:

The bride eyes not her garments,
But her dear Bridegroom's face;
I will not gaze at glory
But on my King of grace;
Not at the crown He giveth,
But on His pierced hand;
The Lamb is all the glory
Of Immanuel's land.[7]

QUESTIONS

1. Isaiah 53:1–12 is another prophetic reflection on the death and resurrection of Christ. How does it develop what we have learned from Psalm 22?
2. 'The goal of missions is the gladness of the peoples in the greatness of

God.' How does this affect the way in which we think about the mission of the church? How should it determine our priorities?

3. The cross of Jesus destroys all human barriers. Why do we keep building them? How can we avoid doing this?

Conclusion:
IT IS FINISHED

The last words uttered in Psalm 22 are: 'He has done it!' (verse 31). The significance of the declaration is clear. It points us forward to and celebrates Christ's accomplishments.

Through the death and resurrection of Christ, the work given to him by his Father has been completed. Derek Kidner comments that verse 31 is 'an announcement not far removed from our Lord's great cry, "It is finished"'.[1]

Jesus lived out this psalm and fulfilled it in the minutest detail. Did he indeed have these words in mind when he spoke the words recorded in John 19:30? 'When he had received the drink, Jesus said, "It is finished." With that, he bowed his head and gave up his spirit.'

The three words, 'It is finished', translate one Greek word, *tetelestai*. Spurgeon says that this word is 'an ocean of meaning in a drop of language ... it would need all the other words ever spoken to explain this one word. It is altogether immeasurable.'[2] In these words Jesus declares that he has finished the work the Father gave him to do. Our debt is paid. God's wrath is spent. Fear becomes hope. Dread becomes joy. Guilt is replaced with gratitude. Satan has been crushed. Prophecy has been fulfilled. Heaven has been guaranteed. Death is dead. Life is assured. Christ has conquered and is alive for ever more.

No matter how long we may have followed Christ, we are all prone to drift from him. We become wandering stars that lose their orbit around the 'sun of Righteousness' (Malachi 4:2). We have to be deliberate and intentional. How do we avoid a cold and formal Christianity? The answer is to stay close to Jesus and his cross. John Stott reminds us of the relationship between the cross and the vitality of our Christian life: 'The Cross is the blazing fire at which the flame of our love is kindled, but we have to get near enough for its sparks to fall on us.'[3]

But we do not come to the cross with a sombre and despondent spirit. We come rejoicing in the fact that Christ is risen from the dead and is alive for ever more. His death and resurrection bring assurance and hope. Our security and identity flow from Calvary and from the empty tomb. This is the anchor our souls desperately need.

I once read the story of a postman who was terrified of a large house with a big dog. The beast looked as if it would eat him alive! But then he noticed that the dog was on a sturdy chain, which was attached to a massive concrete post driven into the ground. The dog might approach him, but it could never reach him. As long as the postman stuck to the path, he was safe. Every morning that he went through the gate, he did not look at the dog or the chain that restrained it. He looked at the post driven into the ground. If it remained unmoved, he was safe.[4]

We walk through a world full of dangers. We need to keep our eyes on Jesus. In his cross and resurrection he is like that post driven into the ground:

> *It is because of [God] that you are in Christ Jesus, who has become for us wisdom from*

> *God – that is, our righteousness, holiness and redemption. Therefore, as it is written: 'Let the one who boasts boast in the Lord'.* (1 Corinthians 1:30–31)

Rightly understood, Psalm 22 gives us a fresh view of these profound realities and should evoke wonder, confidence and praise.

NOTES

1. Finding our way to Calvary

1 Mark Vroegop, *Dark Clouds, Deep Mercy* (Crossway, 2019), p. 21.

2 John Stott, *The Cross of Christ* (IVP, 2006), p. 23.

3 From the hymn 'When I survey the wondrous cross' by Isaac Watts (1707).

2. I am forsaken

1 Matthew Henry, quoted in Frederick Dale Brunner, *The Churchbook: Matthew 13–28* (William B. Eerdmans, 2005), p. 745.

2 John Donne, 'Good Friday, 1613. Riding Westward', lines 17–22, taken from *The Complete John Donne* (Routledge, 2010).

3 C.E.B. Cranfield, quoted in John Stott, *The Cross of Christ*, p. 82.

4 John Stott, *The Cross of Christ*, p. 171.

5 John Piper, *The Passion of the Christ* (Crossway, 2004), p. 21.

6 John Stott, *The Cross of Christ*, p. 165.

7 Alistair Begg, 'Christ-Centred Renewal' from the *Keswick Convention Year Book* (Authentic, 2010), p. 47.

3. I am despised

1 C.H. Spurgeon, *The Treasury of David, Volume 1: Psalms 1–26* (Evangelical Press, 1977), pp. 367–68.

2 *The Orations of Marcus Tullius Cicero*, edited by C.D. Yonge (Covent Garden, 1856), p. 266.

3 From the hymn 'Man of Sorrows, what a name' by Philip P. Bliss (1875).

4 Alan Cole, *Mark: An Introduction and Commentary* (TNTC, 2008), p. 325.

4. I am crucified

1 William Wordsworth, preface to *Lyrical Ballads* (first published in 1802).

2 C.S. Lewis, *Surprised by Joy* (Collins, 2012), p. 226.

3 From the hymn 'All ye that pass by to Jesus draw nigh' by Charles Wesley (1741).

5. *Celebration: He is risen*

1 Derek Kidner, *Psalms 1–72* (IVP, 1973), p. 108.

2 C.S. Lewis, *Miracles* (HarperCollins, 1947), pp. 236–37.

3 C.H. Spurgeon, 'Among us our Beloved stands' (1866): see https://www.praise.org.uk/hymn/among-us-our-beloved-stands/

6. *Proclamation: Jesus is Lord*

1 John Piper, *Let the Nations be Glad* (third edition: Baker, 2010), p. 36.

2 Lesslie Newbigin, quoted in Jonathan Parnell, 'Joy in God Is the Heart of Mission', a blog for Desiring God (9 June, 2011): https://www.desiringgod.org/articles/joy-in-god-is-the-heart-of-mission#:~:text=John%20Piper%20writes%2C,(Psalm%2097%3A1).

3 See Isaiah 53:11–12, the parallel passage to Psalm 22.

4 C.H. Spurgeon, *The Treasury of David, Volume 1*, p. 375.

5 James Johnson, *The Psalms, Volume 1* (Crossway, 2015), pp. 241–42.

6 Jonathan Edwards, *The Christian Pilgrim*, quoted in Alister E. McGrath, *A Brief History of Heaven* (Blackwell, 2003), p. 115.

7 From the hymn 'The sands of time are sinking' by A.R. Cousin (1857).

Conclusion: It is finished

1 Derek Kidner, *Psalms 1–72*, p. 109.

2 C.H. Spurgeon, 'Christ's Dying Word to His Church': see sermon 2344, https://www.thekingdomcollective.com/spurgeon/list/.

3 John Stott, quoted in C.J. Mahaney, *The Cross Centred Life* (Multnomah Press, 2002), p. 55.

4 Taken from the devotional *Food for the Journey* with various contributors (IVP, 2019), p. 679.